ᓄᑕᕋᖅ ᐃᒃᑐᖃᖅᑐᖅ
Baby Signing

ᑎᑎᕋᖅᑐᖅ	Written by
ᕼᐊᓇ ᒋᐳᖅ	Hannah Gifford
ᑎᑎᖅᑐᒐᖅᑐᖅ	Illustrated by
ᐋᓕ ᕼᐃᓐᒡ	Ali Hinch

⊲ċ<
food

ᐊᵘᑲᐃᑦ ᖃᓂᕋᑊᖊᕐᑐᒍ ᓂᕿᒥᕅ
ᐅᕐᑯᒥᖊᕆᕓᑐᐊᕐᑐᑎᑦ.

Bring your hand to your mouth as if
you are putting food in it.

◁L̇L
milk

◁ᒝᒻᑐᑦ ᑎᒍᔭᖅᑐ◁ᕐᑐᑎᑦ.

Open and close your hand as if
squeezing something.

⊲∩̇ᒫ
more

ᗫᑦ ᒍᵡ ᗏᑉ ᒪᗴᗴᑎᑕ ⊲ᑐᑐᑦᑕᑎᑕ ᒍᒥᑉ
⊲ᑫᑐᑦᑕᑎᑉᑭᑕ ᑕᒪᑫᒥᑉ.

Gather your fingertips to your thumbs and
tap both hands together.

CᐱL
all done

ᐃᓂᒪᐃᑦ ᓴᖅᑭᑎᓕᑦᑐᒍ ᐊᑦᒍᑎᑦ
ᓇᑎᖅᒍᑦ ᓴᑎᒧᑐᒥᑦ.

Open your hands with your palms up, and then twist
your wrists quickly so that your palms are facing down.

5

ᐃᑲᔫ

help

ᐊᒡᒐᕗᑦ ᐃᓪᓗᐊ ᐃᒧᑎᓪᓗᒍᑦ ᐃᓪᓗᐊᓄᑦ
ᐊᑦᑐᖅᑎᓪᓗᒍ. ᐃᓪᓗᑦᑐ ᐃᓵᒥᑦ.

Make a fist with one hand and place it on the palm of the other hand. Raise both hands together.

ᐃᒥᕐ
water

ᐸᓂᒃᒪᕐᒃ ᑎᒍᒪᐊᖕᒍᐊᖅᑐᑎᑦ
ᐃᒪᖕᒍᐊᕐᑎᑦ.

Hold your hand as if you are holding a cup
and bring your hand to your mouth.

ᐃᶜᐟ
outside

ᐊᑰᓚᕕᑦ ᐃᶜᑐᐊ ᑎᑐᒥᐊᖅᑎᶜᑐᒍ
ᑭᓇᕕᖅ ᓇᑕᓄᶜ.

Hold your hand in front of your face and move it out a little bit while closing your fingers and thumb together.

ᐱᖖᒍᐊ

play

ᐊᒡᒐᑎᑦ ᑎᒍᒥᐊᖅᑲᑦᑕᐅᑎᓗᑎᒃ ᑭᓯᐊᓂ
ᑯᓪᓘᒃᑭᒃ ᒥᑭᓕᕋᐃᓪᓗ ᐊᓂᖕᒐᑎᓪᓗᒋᑦ.

Hold up both hands with the thumbs and pinky fingers out and twist your wrists.

ᐊᐦᐊ

hurt

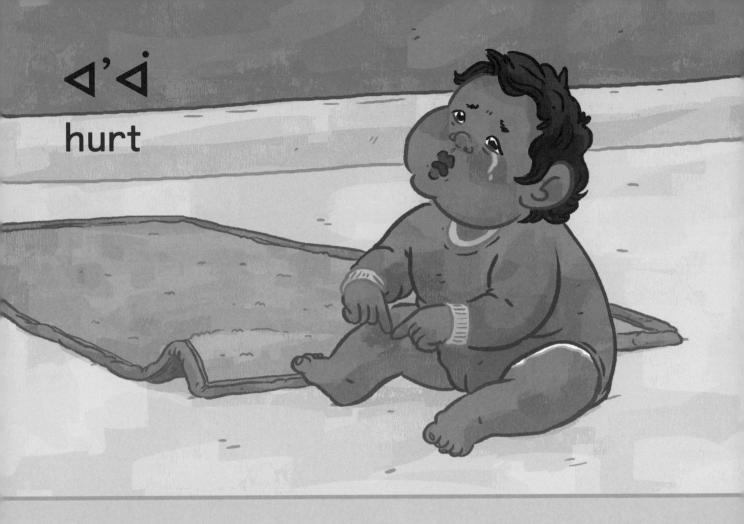

ᒥᑭᓴᕐᖃᐱᖅ ᐊᑦᑐᐊᓐᑎᓗᕆᖅ ᓂᖅᑯᐊᖕᓗᑎᖅᕆᖅ ᐊᖃᓂᐊᕐᒍᖕᑦ.

Tap your index fingers together over the place that hurts.

ᑫᑯᔭᐧᖄᓇᒥᒃ
thank you

ᒪᐅᓇᑎᑦ ᐊᑕᑐᑕᒌᑎᕝᑭᑦ ᑕᐧᒪᕝᓄᑦ
ᐃᕿᓕᖕᒐᑎᕝᓲᕝᑦ.

Touch your fingertips to your chin and
move your hand out.

11

ᐅᖅᑲᓕᒫ
book

ᐊᖕᓇᑎᒃ ᐸᑎᒻᒥᑎᓚᐅᖅᓲᕐᒃ ᐅᖅᑲᓕᒫᓕᖅᑎᑐᒃ
ᒪᐸᐱᖕᒍᐊᖅᑎᒃᕆᑦ.

Hold your hands together and open them, as if you
are opening a book.

ᑐᓕᑦ
bedtime

ᐊᖕᒪᑎᖅ ᐸᑎᒡᒥᑎᑦᑐᒥᕐ ᐅᑐᐊᖁᓂᑦ
ᐊᑦᑐᖅᑎᑦᑐᒥᕐ ᔭᓂᖅᑯᐊᕆᑦ.

Put your palms together and rest them on your
cheek as if you are sleeping.

⊲ȯᴑ
mom

ᐊᑉᓚᓀᑦ ᒪᐸᐱᖅᓚᓀᑦᔪᓯᒃ ᖁᑦᔫᐃᑦ
ᑕᑦᔫᖅᓄᑦ ᐊᑦᑐᑦᑲᓂᒍᒃ.

Tap your thumb to your chin with an
open hand.

ᐊᑖᑕ
dad

ᑯᓪᓗᐃᑦ ᐊᑦᑐᓪᓛᑎᒍᒃ ᖃᐅᖕᓂᑦ ᐊᒡᒐᑎᑦ ᒪᑉᐱᖕᒐᑎᓪᓗᒋᑦ.

Tap your thumb to your forehead with an open hand.

ᐊᕐᑯᓗᖅ
I love you

ᑯᕐᓗᐊᑦ, ᓂᑭᑦ ᒥᕐᓕᕐᕿᐊᑦᓗ
ᐃᖅᖢᖦᑲᑎᕐᓗᑏᑦ.

Hold up your thumb, index finger, and pinky finger.

16